The Iroquois

Liz Sonneborn

Franklin Watts
A Division of Scholastic Inc.
New York • Toronto • London • Auckland • Sydney
Mexico City • New Delhi • Hong Kong
Danbury, Connecticut

Note to readers: Definitions for words in **bold** can be found in the Glossary at the back of this book.

Photographs ©: Albany Institute of History & Art: 36 ("Johnson Hall", by E.L. Henry, oil on canvas, #1993.44); AP/Wide World Photos: 49 (Michael Okoniewski), 46; Art Resource, NY/Smithsonian American Art Museum, Washington, DC: 17; Collection of the New-York Historical Society: 16 (#41012), 20 (#73824), 34 (#7723); Corbis-Bettmann: 35 (Francis G. Mayer), 42; Iroquois Indian Museum, Howes Cave, NY: 6 ("Creations Battle", by John Fadden, #2.016), 10 ("The Grief of Aionwatha", by John Fadden, #2.15), 45 (#3492); North Wind Picture Archives: 8, 22, 23, 24, 25, 27, 29, 32, 38; Photo Researchers, NY/Lawrence Migdale: 48; Raymond Bial: 4, 5; Reinhard Brucker: 14; Richard Alexander Cooke III: 3 right, 12; Rochester Museum & Science Center, Rochester, NY: 9 ("Formation of the League", by Ernest Smith, #MR616); Western History Collections, University of Oklahoma Library, George Long Collection, #8: 40, 41.

Cover illustration by Gary Overacre, interpreted from a photograph from © Art Resources, NY/ Smithsonian American Art Museum, Washington, DC.

Map by XNR Productions Inc.

Library of Congress Cataloging-in-Publication Data

Sonneborn, Liz
    The Iroquois / by Liz Sonneborn
        p. cm — (Watts Library)
    Includes bibliographical references and index.
    ISBN 0-531-11977-7 (lib. bdg.)   0-531-16229-X (pbk.)
    1. Iroquois Indians—Juvenile literature. [1. Iroquois Indians. 2. Indians of North America—New York (State)] I. Title. II. Series.
E99.I7 S66 2002
974.7'0049755–dc21

                                 2001017567

Contents

The Peacemaker left his mother and the land of his people in a canoe. Little did he know of the important role he would play in forming the Iroquois.

Chapter One

The Great Peace

Long ago, a young Huron Indian woman lived alone, isolated from her people. She became pregnant and dreamed that her child would one day do great things. The woman gave birth to a son, who would become known as the **Peacemaker**.

In the Huron people's eyes, the boy acted strangely. He preached to the other children, telling them they should live in peace with one another. The Huron, who respected warriors, were suspicious

Sky Woman and the Twins

The Iroquois explain how the world was created through the story of Sky Woman and her grandsons, Sapling and Flint.

Once, many years ago, the world was covered with water. Only water animals lived there. The sky, however, was the home of the Sky People. One day, Sky Woman fell through a hole in the sky. To make a home for her, Muskrat dove in the water and brought up a paw full of mud. He placed the mud on Turtle's back. It grew into the Earth.

Sky Woman gave birth to a daughter, who had twin boys. Sapling was handsome and good. Flint was ugly and evil. Sapling made straight mountains while Flint made crooked ones. Sapling created corn and tobacco, but his brother made weeds. Sapling made humans while Flint created monsters. Finally, Sapling defeated Flint and sent him to an underground cave. Yet, Flint's presence was still felt, leaving the world full of things both good and bad.

of his message. When the Peacemaker became a man, he built a stone canoe and said goodbye to his mother. He then sailed away, leaving the land of the Huron forever.

The Peacemaker's Vision

The Peacemaker traveled south into a region occupied by five great nations. Similar to the Huron, they were warlike peoples. The tribes not only fought outsiders but also each other. They practiced **blood feuds**. If one tribesperson killed another, the victim's relatives felt bound to take revenge by murdering the killer. The killer's family then felt obligated to retaliate with still another murder. These blood feuds between families never stopped. Each killing led to another, then another, then another.

The Peacemaker wanted to end the blood feuds. As he traveled, he shared his message of peace with the people he met. One day, he came upon a woman who often took in warriors and fed them. She offered food to the Peacemaker as well. After his meal, he told her of his vision of a great peace that would end the fighting between the tribes. She embraced his message and promised not to feed warriors any more. The Peacemaker then gave her a new name. He called her *Jigonhsasee*, meaning "New Face," because she was the first to accept his way of thinking.

The Peacemaker continued on his journey, telling others he met of his vision. While stopping among the Onondaga tribe, he came upon a **longhouse**, the people's traditional dwelling. Holes in the roof of the longhouse let out smoke rising from cooking fires burning inside. Peering through one of the holes, the Peacemaker spied **Hiawatha**. This man had such a disturbed mind that he was a cannibal. The Peacemaker

The Peacemaker looked inside a longhouse and discovered Hiawatha.

told Hiawatha his message of peace, and Hiawatha's mind was cleared.

The Peacemaker soon traveled to the lands of the Mohawk people. But before leaving, he assigned a task to Hiawatha.

The Song of Hiawatha

One of the most famous poems in American literature is *The Song of Hiawatha*. It was written by Henry Wadsworth Longfellow in 1855. The poem, however, is not about the great founder of the Iroquois Confederacy. Longfellow based his work on the writings of Henry Rowe Schoolcraft. Schoolcraft mistakenly gave the name "Hiawatha" to Nanabozho, a hero in the legends of the Ojibwa Indians who lived in the Great Lakes region.

Hiawatha would have to convince Thadodaho, an Onondaga medicine man, to embrace the Peacemaker's words. Convincing Thadodaho would be difficult. Thadodaho's mind was so twisted that he used his power for evil. As evidence of his viciousness, Thadodaho's hair was full of slithering snakes.

When the Peacemaker reached Mohawk territory, he climbed a tree that overlooked a great cavern. The Mohawk cut down the tree, but the next morning to their amazement, they found the Peacemaker sitting quietly by a fire. They realized that, to survive the fall, the Peacemaker had to be very powerful. They listened to his words, and became the first of the five tribes to agree to live in peace.

In the meantime, Hiawatha's efforts to convert Thadodaho brought him great grief. One by one, the evil Thadodaho killed Hiawatha's three daughters. Hiawatha was devastated by his loss until he found some shell beads. He strung them on three strings to represent his sorrow. The Peacemaker then came upon Hiawatha. His powerful words dried Hiawatha's tears and cleared his troubled mind.

The Peacemaker and Hiawatha meet with Thadodaho to convince him to stop warring with other tribes.

9

Spreading the Word

Together, the Peacemaker and Hiawatha set out to visit the Oneida tribe to the west. They preached the Peacemaker's message, which the Oneida embraced. They then continued on, passing through Onondaga territory to the lands of the Cayuga and the Seneca. Both tribes also accepted their teachings. Now only Thadodaho of the Onondaga stood in their way of creating a league between the five tribes.

The Peacemaker and Hiawatha traveled to Thadodaho's home to make another appeal. This time, Hiawatha combed the snakes from Thadodaho's hair so that his mind was no longer twisted. They asked Thadodaho to support them, offering him an honored place among the tribes' leaders. Thadodaho at last agreed to let the Onondaga join, and a great league of tribes was born.

This painting shows Hiawatha grieving for his three daughters. In his hand he holds the strings of shell beads.

This is just one version of the story of how the **Iroquois Confederacy** started. This confederacy originally included five tribes—the Mohawk, Oneida, Onondaga, Cayuga, and Seneca—who lived in what is now the state of New York. The confederacy was probably founded between 1400 and 1500, at least one hundred years before these tribes came in contact with Europeans.

The founding of the Iroquois Confederacy was a major event in the history of North America. By agreeing to live in peace with one another, these five tribes not only ended their blood feuds. They also created a powerful Indian alliance—one that would rule what is now the northeastern United States for nearly three hundred years.

The Iroquois Confederacy

The original confederacy was also known as the Iroquois League or the Five Nations.

This building is an example of a traditional longhouse. The fencing in the foreground is designed to keep intruders out of the village.

Chapter Two

The Longhouse People

In the Iroquois's own language, they called themselves the **Hodenosaunee**, or "People of the Longhouse." Longhouses were homes made by placing elm-bark shingles over a frame of bent saplings. Most were about 25 feet (8 meters) wide and 80 feet (24 m) long, with living space for about 50 inhabitants. The largest longhouses, however, stretched up to

400 feet (121 m) and housed more than 100 people. Each village consisted of a cluster of between 30 and 150 longhouses, all surrounded by a high fence of wooden poles to keep out intruders.

Each longhouse had two entrances at the narrow sides. Inside, family living quarters were set up along the two long walls. A row of small fires down the middle were used to cook food and warm the house. Small holes were left in the roof to let smoke out and sunlight in.

For the Iroquois, the longhouse was more than just a comfortable home. It was also a symbol. Just as the families in a longhouse dwelled side by side in harmony, the five Iroquois nations lived in peace in their adjoining territories.

This photograph shows the interior of a traditional longhouse.

The Iroquois Way

Above the doors of each longhouse, the inhabitants hung an image of an animal, such as a turtle, wolf, or bear. These animals represented the **clan** of the people who lived there. A clan was a group of relatives who believed they shared the same common ancestor. Clan members felt an obligation to help one another. For instance, if a hunter of the Turtle Clan was traveling through the woods and came upon a Turtle Clan longhouse, the people living there would be expected to take him in and feed him.

Iroquois Indians belonged to the same clan as their mothers. When they married, they had to choose a spouse from another clan. After marrying, a young man left his mother's longhouse and moved in with his wife's family. His new longhouse was managed by its clan mothers—elder women who were considered very wise.

In general, women were highly respected by the Iroquois. They were particularly revered because of their role as farmers. Near each village, Iroquois men cleared fields, which women then planted with corn, beans, and squash. These crops—called the **Three Sisters**—provided the Iroquois with most of their food. They could be eaten fresh, or dried for later use. With the food women harvested, the Iroquois could almost always be sure of having enough to eat throughout the cold winter.

In addition to farming, women gathered nuts, berries, and greens that grew wild on their land. For instance, they picked wild strawberries, dried them in the sun, and added them to batter to make sweet bread. They also used the sap of maple trees to flavor a tasty mush made from pounded corn and water.

Men added to the food supply by hunting deer, bears, and other animals that roamed the forest. Their favorite hunting tools were bows and arrows, but they also caught animals in snares. The Iroquois were clever fishermen too. They crafted

On the far left, an Iroquois woman gathers sap from a maple tree while the other women perform different chores.

all kinds of hooks and nets to catch fish in the many rivers and lakes in their territory.

Iroquois men were also proud of being great warriors. Although they did not fight one another, the Iroquois tribes constantly warred with other peoples. They often raided enemies' villages to steal food and take prisoners. Some captives were tortured and killed, while others were adopted into their tribes.

If a war party suffered even one **casualty**, everyone in the village mourned. The relatives of a dead warrior covered

their faces and clothing with ashes to show their sorrow. Friends tried to console them, while they washed and dressed the body for burial. Food and treasured items, such as a tobacco pipe or a favorite bowl, were also placed in the grave. Relatives mourned the death of loved ones so deeply that the name of a dead person was often not used for years. Once their grief faded, the name was given to a newborn, in whom the dead person's spirit was thought to live again.

This 1831 painting is a portrait of a Seneca warrior. The Iroquois were known for being strong and fierce warriors.

Honoring the Spirits

To keep their world in order, the Iroquois performed age-old ceremonies and rituals. One of the most important was the Green Corn Festival. It was held each summer when the corn, beans, and squash were ripe and ready for harvest. Through dances and feasts, the Iroquois celebrated the Creator who had blessed them with these foods. They also gave thanks to supernatural beings who helped them throughout their lives.

In late January or early February, when men came home from the fall hunt, the Iroquois performed the Mid-Winter Ceremony. On the first day of this ritual, elder men went from longhouse to longhouse. They told each family to clean their home and stir the ashes of their house fire. In the days that followed, the villagers came together to dance and recite a prayer of thanksgiving.

During the Mid-Winter Ceremony, they also performed a ritual of dream-guessing. The Iroquois believed that dreams revealed a person's innermost desires. They thought that if these desires were not met, a person could become ill. In the dream-guessing ritual, people who had experienced an unsettling dream asked others to guess what they had dreamed about. When someone guessed correctly, that person had to fulfill the dreamer's desire. For instance, once in the 1700s, a troubled old woman dreamed that she presented a family with a hoe. The family guessed rightly that she wanted land. Once its members gave her a small plot, the woman's mind was set at ease.

Stone Giants

The Iroquois told stories of evil giants made of stone who wandered around the countryside, looking for people to eat. These monsters were greatly feared, since they could not be hurt by spears or arrows.

False Faces

Beginning in the 1500s, Iroquois healers often wore ceremonial wooden masks called **False Faces**. Many False Faces featured a twisted mouth, a wild tuft of horse hair, and a crooked nose. These masks honored Shagody-owehgowah. The Iroquois said that this great giant once challenged the Creator to see who had the power to move a mountain. The Creator won the competition. The mountain he moved smacked into Shagody-owehgowah's face, pushing his nose to one side.

The Iroquois also looked to healers to keep their minds and bodies healthy. Using more than two hundred different plants, Iroquois healers made homemade medicines to treat everything from snakebites to broken limbs to a lovesick heart. Some also practiced cures for illnesses that the Iroquois believed were brought on by witchcraft. These medicine men and women sang special songs to combat the witches' evil. Often, healers sucked on portions of their patients' bodies, then pulled stones or other small objects out of their mouths. They then declared that witches had used these objects to make their patients sick.

The Great Council

Like healers, chiefs were held in high regard by the Iroquois. Each village had its own council of chiefs, who made decisions about local matters. For business affecting the Iroquois Confederacy as a whole, however, the Iroquois looked to the **Great Council** for leadership. The Great Council had

Chief Hendrick holds one of the Iroquois wampum belts used to record important events.

forty-eight members and met at Onondaga, which was located in the middle of Iroquois territory. Each position was named after one of the original council members. A forty-ninth seat was named for Hiawatha, but because of his importance in the founding of the confederacy, this position was never filled. To give an even greater honor to the Peacemaker, his seat on the council was retired after his death.

Although council members were always men, clan mothers held the real power. If a chief behaved badly or did not obey the clan mothers, they could take away his position. Thus, the former chief was humiliated in the eyes of his people.

The decisions of the Great Council were often recorded using **wampum**. Wampum were white and purple beads made from sea shells. To commemorate significant events, these beads were strung into wide belts. The wisest elders used the designs as memory aids to help them remember long rituals, stories, and treaties. The most important wampum belts were stored at Onondaga. There, a special wampum keeper was responsible for the safekeeping of these treasured reminders of the great history of the Iroquois.

The Longest Wampum Belt

The Washington Covenant Belt, which commemorated a peace treaty between the Iroquois and the United States, was made up of about ten thousand beads.

The Iroquois learned Europeans would give them tools and pots in exchange for animal furs.

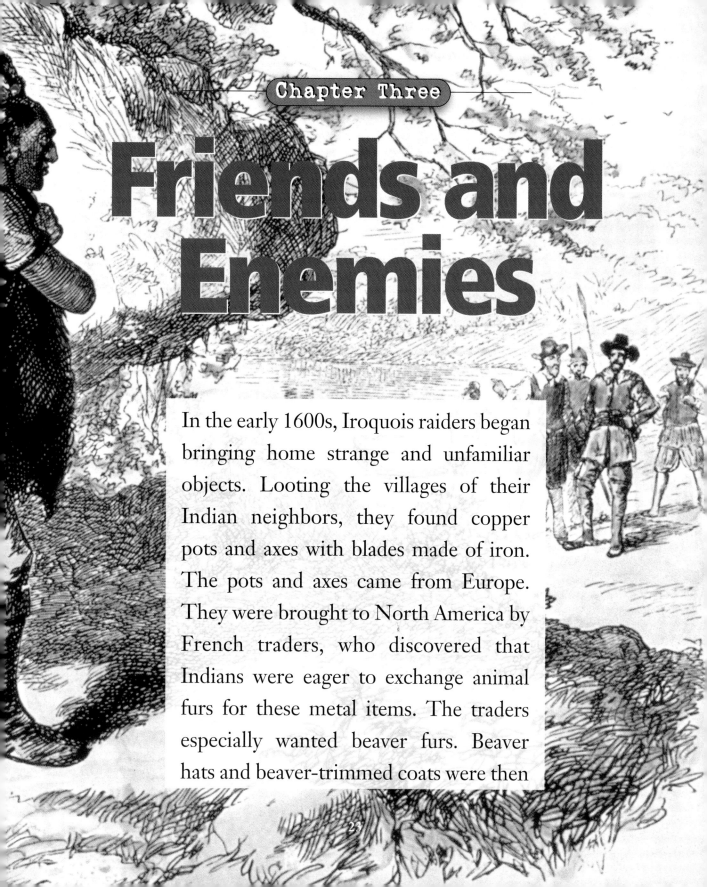

Chapter Three

Friends and Enemies

In the early 1600s, Iroquois raiders began bringing home strange and unfamiliar objects. Looting the villages of their Indian neighbors, they found copper pots and axes with blades made of iron. The pots and axes came from Europe. They were brought to North America by French traders, who discovered that Indians were eager to exchange animal furs for these metal items. The traders especially wanted beaver furs. Beaver hats and beaver-trimmed coats were then popular in Europe. When the traders traveled home, they could make fortunes by selling these furs for high prices.

The Fur Trade

To make money from the **fur trade**, the French king created a **colony** in North America called New France. It was headed by Samuel de Champlain. Champlain helped build a trading partnership with the Algonquin and Huron Indians. These tribes insisted that Champlain help them fight their Indian enemies—particularly the Mohawk, the Iroquois tribe living closest to the French colony.

On July 30, 1609, Champlain, two other Frenchmen, and about sixty Algonquin, Montagnais, and Huron warriors

Samuel de Champlain easily defeated the Mohawk by using a weapon that was new to the tribe—the gun.

attacked several hundred Mohawk near what is now Lake Champlain. As the battle began, Champlain, wearing full metal armor, stepped forward and fired a gun. He shot three Mohawk war leaders, killing two instantly and fatally wounding the third. The rest of the Mohawk were stunned. They had never seen a gun before and were thrown into a panic. Champlain's forces quickly defeated them, killing more than fifty warriors. For decades after the Battle of Lake Champlain, the Mohawk considered the French their bitter enemies.

Fortunately for the Mohawk, they could deal with other European traders to obtain metal goods and guns. The Dutch established a trading post along the Hudson River in present-day eastern New York. The Dutch first traded with the nearby

While the Mohawk hated the French, they did become allies with the Dutch.

Mahican Indians, the Mohawk's longtime enemies. The Mohawk began battling the Mahican to get access to Dutch trade items. In 1643, the Mohawk finally made a formal alliance with the Dutch. Soon European goods were flowing to all the Iroquois nations.

In many ways, these European objects made life for the Iroquois better. Metal tools were sharper and more durable than ones they made from stone and bones. Guns were more effective weapons than bows and arrows, both on the hunt and in battle. Yet, these items came at a high price. Europeans also brought with them diseases that had been unknown in North America, such as measles and smallpox. Like other Indians, the Iroquois had no natural defenses to these diseases, so when they caught them they often died.

The fur trade also made warfare more frequent and more deadly. In the past, Iroquois men went to war to raid their enemies' villages, take a few prisoners, and gain the respect of their people. Now they battled other Indians to get rid of trade competitors and take over their hunting grounds. Their determination to rule the fur trade soon led the Iroquois into the bloodiest wars they had ever known.

Expanding the Iroquois World

By the 1640s, the Iroquois were focusing much of their wrath on the Huron Indians. The French-allied Huron lived to the northwest in what is now southern Ontario, Canada. They had grown rich in the fur trade by acting as middlemen.

A Deadly Disease

In 1634, smallpox swept through Mohawk territory. Within a few months, disease killed more than half the tribe.

Through trade, they obtained thick furs from northern Indian hunters. The Huron then traded the furs to the French for a hefty profit. Jealous of the Huron's success, the Iroquois were desperate to drive them out of business.

Heavily armed with Dutch guns, a large Seneca army set upon the Huron village of Teanaostaiaé in early July 1648. About seven hundred Huron were killed or captured and much of their food stores and fields were destroyed. Another

The Iroquois envied the success of the Huron and fought them to destroy their fur trade business.

thousand escaped, but they were left without food or homes for the winter.

The next year, the Iroquois continued their war against the now starving Huron. They made a surprise attack on Taenhatentaron and destroyed the village. Three men escaped and warned the other Huron about the invasion. The Huron fought valiantly. The Iroquois suffered so many casualties that, after taking two more villages, they were ready to retreat. By that time, though, the Huron had given up hope. They fled from their homeland, splitting off into small groups. Some were absorbed by other Indian groups, including the Iroquois. The Huron would never again live as a united people.

Hoping to expand their hunting territory even farther, the Iroquois moved against other western tribes. They waged war against the Petun, Neutral, and Erie, driving these groups off their lands just as they had the Huron. By 1657, the Iroquois had destroyed all their French-allied Indian rivals to the north and west. By adopting thousands of prisoners taken in war, they had also grown in number. Strong and powerful, the Iroquois were now the unchallenged Indian leaders in the fur trade.

A Neutral Stance

Even with these astounding victories, the mighty Iroquois were still vulnerable, especially as tensions within the confederacy began to rise. In 1653, the Iroquois negotiated a peace with their old French enemies. Trading with the French brought the Iroquois more European goods than ever before,

The Wyandot

One branch of the surviving Huron became known as the Wyandot. Today, they live in northeastern Oklahoma.

but the Mohawk became bitter. They thought the Onondaga were getting special treatment from the French. The Mohawk were particularly angry that the French sent priests to Onondaga to **convert** the Indians to Christianity. The Mohawk saw this as evidence that the French favored their Onondaga kin.

For other reasons, many Onondaga also were angry at the priests who they thought were witches. The priests annoyed the Indians by trying to force them to stop practicing their own religious ceremonies. As their relationship with the Onondaga soured, the priests feared for their lives. As part of

The Onondaga rejected the French missionaries' efforts to convert them to Christianity.

an escape plan, they held a feast for the Onondaga. While the Indians slept off their heavy meal, the priests slipped away into the night.

The Iroquois also faced trouble on the war front. After conquering the tribes to their west, they set their sights on the hunting grounds of the Susquehannock to the south. These Indians were skilled warriors and were armed with plenty of guns. After twenty years, the Iroquois were finally able to defeat them. But their own losses were extremely high.

In addition, their new French allies proved to be a continual threat. In the 1660s, the Mohawk started attacking French-allied tribes in the Great Lakes region. To punish them, a French army invaded Mohawk territory and destroyed one of their villages in 1666.

By this time, the Iroquois had another European power to deal with. In 1664, the English took over the Dutch colony of New Netherland and renamed it New York. The English sought allegiance with the powerful Iroquois. Relations with the French, however, continued to be strained. By 1680, the Iroquois had launched a savage war against the Miami, Illinois, and Ottawa—western tribes allied to the French. In retaliation, the French repeatedly attacked the Iroquois. Then, in 1696, the Ojibwa, Ottawa, and Potawatomi—calling themselves the Council of Three Fires—defeated the invading Iroquois and drove them out of their lands.

The Iroquois had grown exhausted by this constant fighting. In 1701, they finally negotiated a peace agreement with

The Six Nations

In the 1722, the Tuscarora joined the Iroquois Confederacy—making the Five Nations into the Six Nations. Distant relatives of the Iroquois tribes, the Tuscarora traditionally lived in what are now North and South Carolina. In the early 1700s, however, English settlers tried to push them from their lands, and the Tuscarora fought back. The Tuscarora lost the war with the settlers and fled north to Iroquois territory. The tribe settled among the Oneida before becoming a member of the Iroquois League.

the French, while retaining good relations with the English. The Iroquois then discovered that refusing to pledge complete allegiance to either nation put them in a powerful position. Both the French and English were eager to stay in their good favor, so the Iroquois could play them off one another. For a time, this strategy worked. After a century of warfare, the Iroquois now had a chance to rebuild their nations as the English and French competed for their friendship.

While most of the Iroquois joined the French in the French and Indian War, some of the Mohawk took the English side.

Chapter Four

Fighting for Survival

In the early 1700s, France and England fought several wars for control over lands in North America. Their final conflict was called the French and Indian War (1754–1763), because most Indians who took part in the war fought on the side of the French.

Some Mohawk, however, sided with the British. They were friends of William Johnson, an English trader and official who had been adopted into the tribe. With the help of the Mohawk, the British

33

Chief Hendrick

Though more than seventy years old, Chief Hendrick of the Mohawk courageously fought and died alongside English troops during the French and Indian War.

won the war and ordered France to give up its claims in North America.

The French defeat quickly proved a problem for the confederacy as a whole. The Iroquois were accustomed to making the English bow to their demands by threatening to support the French. With the French gone, the Iroquois no longer had the same control over the English. The confederacy was soon losing their influence over Indians and non-Indians alike.

Taking Sides

The situation grew even worse for the Iroquois as English settlers—calling themselves Americans—headed toward war with their own country. Under the influence of William Johnson, the Mohawk vowed to stay loyal to England. The Oneida and Tuscarora, however, were friendly with a missionary named Samuel Kirkland. He pushed them to side with the Americans.

In 1776, fighting broke out between the American colonists and the English. The Iroquois tribes could not agree on which side to support. The Mohawk, Seneca, Cayuga, and Onondaga chose the English. The Oneida and Tuscarora chose the Americans. In the past, the tribes of the confederacy had disagreed over specific issues. But never before had such a disagreement meant that they would face each other on the battlefield.

General George Washington sent American troops to invade the lands of the Seneca, Cayuga, and Onondaga in western Iroquois territory in 1779. Their soldiers destroyed nearly all these tribes' villages and burned their fields. Many western Iroquois were left homeless and starving. As many as half of their people died during the war.

The Albany Plan of Union

In 1754, statesman Benjamin Franklin proposed a plan for governing the thirteen American colonies modeled after the Iroquois Confederacy.

Once again, the Iroquois became divided by war. Some fought for the English while others joined the American side in the Revolutionary War.

Molly Brant

One of the most powerful Iroquois women of the 1700s was Mohawk Molly Brant. For many years, she shared a huge mansion (shown above) with William Johnson, an English official respected by her tribe. When the Revolutionary War broke out, she rallied Mohawk warriors, including her brother Joseph, to fight for the English. An observer noted that, among the Mohawk, one word from Molly Brant had more influence "than a thousand from any white man."

The American campaign made the pro-English Iroquois furious. In retaliation, raiders led by Mohawk leader Joseph Brant attacked American settlements, destroying food and supplies that might be used by the American forces. They also attacked the villages of the Oneida and Tuscarora because these tribes still supported the Americans.

The Revolutionary War was a disaster for the Iroquois. Not only were many of their villages destroyed and their people killed, but the confederacy was also left in shambles. The great peace of Hiawatha and the Peacemaker was broken as Iroquois battled Iroquois.

A Divided Nation

The war's end brought the Iroquois little relief. In 1783, the English signed the Treaty of Paris, in which they admitted defeat. In the treaty, however, they made no provisions to protect their Iroquois allies. The pro-English Iroquois would have to face the Americans' wrath with no help from England.

Some English officials were embarrassed by the government's treatment of their Indian friends. They pushed their country to set aside a tract of English-held land on the Grand River in present-day Ontario, Canada. Joseph Brant led many of his Mohawk followers to the Grand River lands, which became a **reserve** known as Six Nations. Most of the other Iroquois, however, chose to stay in their homelands.

To punish the pro-English Iroquois, the new United States government forced them to sign the Treaty of Fort Stanwix in 1784. Through this agreement, the Indians gave up lands in western New York, Pennsylvania, and Ohio. In one stroke, these tribes lost most of the territory they had won by battling their Indian enemies.

In the years that followed, Iroquois leaders sold much of their remaining lands to New York state officials and land companies. In the short term, the deals brought money into the tribes. In the long term, though, they chipped away at the

After the Revolutionary War, the Iroquois lost or sold much of their lands, leaving them only a few small reservations to call home.

Iroquois's power as their territory shrank smaller and smaller. By 1800, most Iroquois were living on a few small **reservations** in New York State and reserves in Canada. Soon, their old hunting grounds were covered with the cabins of settlers.

Reservation Life

Living on reservations proved difficult for many Iroquois, particularly men. Women could still take pride in their work as farmers and caregivers. But men, confined within reservation borders, could no longer earn respect as hunters and warriors. Some became consumed by feelings of worthlessness and despair.

The Longhouse Religion

In June 1799, a Seneca man named Handsome Lake collapsed. He was a heavy drinker, and alcohol had taken a terrible toll on his health. His relatives assumed he was dead.

To their shock, hours later, Handsome Lake suddenly came back to life. He said he had seen an amazing vision. Four messengers, dressed in Indian clothing, appeared before him. They gave him a message from the Creator, which set down rules for how the Iroquois should live. In the next few months, Handsome Lake had two more visions, during which he received more instructions.

For the rest of his life, he preached what he had learned. He told his people to give up alcohol, witchcraft, and gambling. He also encouraged them to strengthen their family ties, perform old ceremonies, and adopt many non-Indian ways. Handsome Lake's teachings, which became known as the **Longhouse Religion,** are still observed by many Iroquois today.

For relief from the stress of reservation life, many Iroquois turned to religion. Some became followers of Handsome Lake, a Seneca prophet who taught a new religion that combined traditional beliefs and non-Indian customs. Others looked to Christian **missionaries** who came to their lands. Quakers, Methodists, Baptists, and Catholics all ministered to the Iroquois. Largely because of the efforts of a Mohawk named Eleazar Williams, many of the Oneida became Episcopalian converts.

In 1823, Williams led his supporters to a new reservation near present-day Green Bay, Wisconsin. Under pressure from whites, a group of Seneca and Cayuga in Ohio also moved west to lands in Indian Territory (now Oklahoma) in 1831.

These Seneca and Wyandot children in the first to eight grades attended the Seneca Indian School in 1887.

Other Iroquois, however, resisted non-Indians' continued demands for their traditional lands.

The Seneca, for instance, became furious when they learned of the Treaty of Buffalo Creek of 1838. In this agreement, a small group of Seneca leaders were bribed into selling the tribes' four reservations in New York for land in present-day Kansas. With the help of Quaker missionaries, the Seneca negotiated for the return of two reservations—Allegany and Cattaraugus. Ten years later, the Iroquois living

there overthrew their old chiefs and decided to start electing their leaders.

Throughout the 1800s, the Iroquois saw many changes to their way of life. They began to wear non-Indian clothes and live in cabins instead of longhouses. Following the example of whites, many Iroquois men started taking over the farming duties their wives used to perform. Their children began going to school, where they learned to read and write in English. In many ways, the lives of the Iroquois came to resemble those of their non-Indian neighbors. Yet they remembered their traditions and the ways of their ancestors. Though scattered in communities far and wide, in their hearts and minds they remained Iroquois.

Many Iroquois left their reservations to find jobs. Some Mohawk Indians went to work building skyscrapers in Manhattan.

Chapter Five

The Modern Iroquois

In the 1900s, the Iroquois continued to experience changes in their lives. Over time, many moved from farming into other professions. Some became laborers working for wages. One of the most popular professions was construction work. Mohawk men became famous for their skill and fearlessness in walking along high steel beams while building enormous skyscrapers. Other Iroquois took advantage of better educational opportunities to become teachers, lawyers, doctors, government workers, and other professionals. Among them were Oneida Robert L. Bennett and Mohawk-Sioux Louis R. Bruce. During the 1960s and 1970s, they each served as commissioner of Indian affairs, the head of the U.S. government agency assigned to deal with all American Indian groups.

Iroquois people sometimes had to move away from their reservations and reserves to take these new jobs. For instance, large communities of Iroquois grew up in Buffalo and Rochester in western New York and in the Brooklyn section of New York City. Even when Iroquois workers became city residents, many kept close ties to their people. They often returned to their old communities to visit relatives and attend traditional ceremonies.

Onondaga Athlete Tom Longboat

In 1907, Onondaga long-distance runner Tom Longboat won the Boston Marathon, beating the previous record time by five minutes.

Losing Ground

Unfortunately for the Iroquois, one thing that did not change in the 1900s was the constant demand for their land. In the 1950s, the Seneca were sent into a panic as the U.S. Army Corps of Engineers made plans to construct the Kinzua Dam. This project would flood their entire Cornplanter Reservation in Pennsylvania and part of the Allegany Reservation in New York. In an effort to persuade the government to abandon the Kinzua Dam, Seneca leaders spoke out in newspapers and on television. The leaders earned the sympathy and support of many non-Indians, but the Army Corps of Engineers began working on the dam anyway. As a result, 9,000 acres (3,642

hectares) of the best Seneca land was destroyed, and 130 Seneca Indians were forced from their homes.

In 1958, the Tuscarora launched a similar battle against the New York State Power Authority. The company wanted

This photograph shows what the site of the Kinzua Dam looked like during construction in 1963.

The Border Crossing Celebration

In the Jay Treaty of 1794, the Iroquois were given the right "freely to pass and repass" the border between the United States and Canada. When the U.S. government challenged this right in 1924, Iroquois activists went into action, eventually forcing Congress to recognize their treaty rights. To celebrate this victory, each July a crowd of Iroquois proudly marches across the international border at Niagara Falls during the Border Crossing Celebration.

A four-year-old Tuscarora boy holds a sign objecting to the New York State Power Authority's plan to take over Tuscarora land.

to take over part of the Tuscarora's reservation to build a reservoir. The Tuscarora hired lawyers to stop the construction. While the case was still in court, power authority workers began arriving on the reservation. In a mass demonstration, the Tuscarora men, women, and children, with protest signs in hand, blocked the workers' path. The protesters even lay down in front of the trucks to keep them doing any work. In the end, however, the U.S. Supreme Court ruled in favor of the power authority, and the Tuscarora lost their land.

Fighting Back

Despite these defeats, Iroquois activists learned much from their experiences. They found out how to make their voices heard in the courts and in the press. Using these lessons, the Oneida in 1985 argued before the U.S. Supreme Court that New York State illegally took 250,000 acres (101,000 hectares) from the tribe in the 1700s. Agreeing with the tribe, the Court ordered that the Oneida could sue New York State for their land losses. The hallmark case has inspired other Indian groups to sue for land taken from them hundreds of years ago.

In 1990, the Mohawk of the Kanesatake Reserve chose protesting as a means to spotlight their grievances. That summer, they focused the world's attention on the small town of Oka in Quebec, Canada. There, armed Mohawk activists took over the entrance of a forest. The Mohawk were angry because the mayor of Oka had approved a plan for building a golf course on forestland, which the Mohawk claimed they owned. For months, Canadian police surrounded the protesters. One officer was shot before the standoff ended. The land dispute that sparked the violence at Oka is still not fully resolved.

Unfortunately, recent arguments among the Mohawk on New York's Akwesasne Reservation have also ended in violence. There, traditionalists who opposed gambling fought with other Mohawk who wanted to open casinos on the reservation. In 1990, two men were killed in gunfire exchanged between the two sides. In the end, the pro-gambling forces won. The Akwesasne Mohawk Casino opened in 1999.

Keeping Traditions Alive

In addition to fighting for their land and their rights, today's Iroquois have worked hard to retain their old ways and beliefs. Several Iroquois reservations and reserves have established museums to share information about their culture with Indian and non-Indian visitors. Many Iroquois have also campaigned for the return of sacred objects held in other museums' collections. The Iroquois rejoiced in 1989 when the New York State Museum returned twelve wampum belts. They were placed in the care of the Onondaga, the traditional keepers of the wampum belts.

Children at the Onondaga Nation reservation play lacrosse—a sport that is very popular with many Iroquois.

Another living tradition of the Iroquois is the game of lacrosse. The Iroquois have played this Indian sport for hundreds of years. In 1983, they formed the Iroquois National Lacrosse Club. Thirteen years later, the club won permission from the International Lacrosse Federation to compete as a national team. The Iroquois Nationals now participate in world championships, playing teams representing the United States, Canada, Japan, and other nations.

Art—both traditional and contemporary—also remains an important part of the Iroquois world. Like their ancestors, artisans still carve False Faces and weave cornhusk baskets and dolls. Other artists,

Joanne Shenandoah, an Oneida, mixes traditional melodies and chants with contemporary musical styles.

such as Seneca painter Ernest Smith and Mohawk painter Richard Glazer Danay, have won renown working in non-Indian art forms. Modern Iroquois, too, have made their mark on the performing arts. Oneida stage and screen actor Graham Greene, for instance, was nominated for an Academy Award for his supporting role in the film *Dances with Wolves* (1990). Equally distinguished is singer-songwriter Joanne Shenandoah. Also an Oneida, her music, drawing on traditional Iroquois songs, earned her the title Best Female Artist at the first annual Native American Music Awards in 1997.

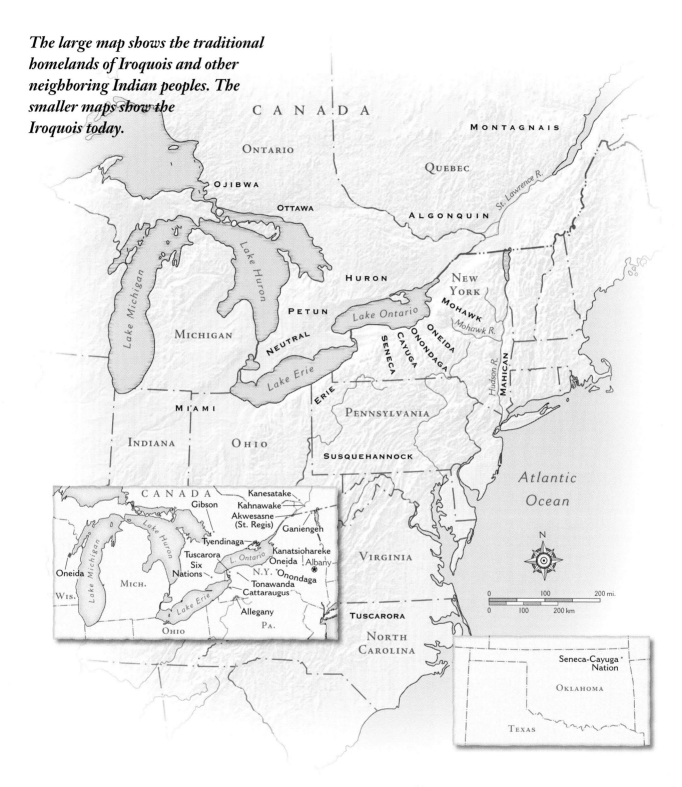

The large map shows the traditional homelands of Iroquois and other neighboring Indian peoples. The smaller maps show the Iroquois today.

CANADA

MONTAGNAIS

ONTARIO

QUEBEC

OJIBWA

OTTAWA

ALGONQUIN

St. Lawrence R.

HURON

NEW YORK

MOHAWK

Lake Ontario

Mohawk R.

ONEIDA

ONONDAGA

CAYUGA

Lake Michigan

Lake Huron

PETUN

SENECA

MICHIGAN

NEUTRAL

Hudson R.

MAHICAN

Lake Erie

ERIE

MI'AMI

PENNSYLVANIA

INDIANA

OHIO

SUSQUEHANNOCK

Atlantic Ocean

CANADA

Kanesatake

Gibson

Kahnawake

Akwesasne (St. Regis)

Ganiengeh

Tyendinaga

Lake Michigan

Lake Huron

L. Ontario

Kanatsiohareke

Tuscarora

Oneida

Albany

Oneida

Six Nations

N.Y.

Onondaga

MICH.

WIS.

Tonawanda

Cattaraugus

Lake Erie

Allegany

PA.

OHIO

VIRGINIA

N

TUSCARORA

NORTH CAROLINA

0   100   200 mi.
0   100   200 km

Seneca-Cayuga Nation

OKLAHOMA

TEXAS

50

Today, there are seventy thousand Iroquois living in the United States and Canada. On the surface, the lives of most Iroquois are like those of their non-Indian neighbors. They wear the same kinds of clothes, live in the same kinds of houses, listen to the same kinds of music, and watch the same television shows as other contemporary North Americans. But, underneath, the culture of their ancestors continues to guide and nourish them. While living in the modern world, the Iroquois remain the People of the Longhouse—full of pride in their past and hope for their future.

The American Iroquois

According to the 1990 census, the Iroquois are the eighth largest Indian group in the United States.

Timeline

c. 1400 to 1500	The Peacemaker and Hiawatha establish the Iroquois Confederacy.
1609	Samuel de Champlain and his Indian allies battle the Mohawk at Lake Champlain.
1634	Smallpox epidemic spreads through Iroquois territory.
1643	The Mohawk negotiate peace with the Dutch.
1644	The English take over Dutch territory and make allies of the Iroquois.
1645	The Mohawk make a peace with the French and their Algonquin and Huron allies.
1648–49	The Iroquois wage war on the Huron, destroying them as a unified tribe.
1696	The Ojibwa, Ottawa, and Potawatomi drive the Iroquois from their territory.
1701	The Iroquois renew peace with the French.
1722	The Tuscarora join the Iroquois Confederacy.
1754–63	The Mohawk aid the British during the French and Indian War.
1776	The Revolutionary War disrupts the Iroquois Confederacy. The Seneca, Cayuga, Onondaga, and Mohawk side with England and the Oneida and Tuscarora side with the United States.
1779	U.S. troops invade Seneca, Cayuga, and Onondaga territory.
1784	The pro-English Mohawk move to the Six Nations Reserve in Ontario, Canada.

1784	The treaty of Fort Stanwix forces the Iroquois to give up their land in New York, Pennsylvania, and Ohio.
1799	The Seneca prophet Handsome Lake establishes the Longhouse Religion.
1823	Oneida faction moves to present-day Wisconsin.
1831	Group of Seneca and Cayuga relocate to Indian Territory.
1838	Seneca chiefs give up New York reservations in the Treaty of Buffalo Creek.
1928	U.S. Congress confirms the right of the Iroquois to cross the United States–Canada border freely.
1956–65	Construction of the Kinzua Dam floods the Seneca's Cornplanter and Allegany reservations.
1960	Tuscarora lose their battle to stop the New York State Power Authority from building a reservoir on tribal land.
1985	U.S. Supreme Court acknowledges the Oneida's right to sue New York state.
1989	New York State Museum returns twelve wampum belts to the Iroquois.
1990	The Akwesasne Mohawk stage a protest at Oka, Quebec.

Glossary

blood feud—a long-standing, violent quarrel between two families

casualty—a person who is wounded or killed in war

clan—a group of relatives within a tribe

colony—an area settled by foreigners from a distant territory or country

convert—to persuade someone to adopt another religion

False Faces—carved wooden masks worn by Iroquois healers during curing rituals

fur trade—the trade network, in which Indians gave animal furs to Europeans in exchange for guns, metal tools, and other goods made in Europe

Great Council—the governing body of the Iroquois Confederacy

Hiawatha—a legendary Iroquois figure who helped the Peacemaker establish the Iroquois Confederacy

Hodenosaunee—the name that the Iroquois call themselves, meaning "People of the Longhouse"

Iroquois Confederacy—the alliance formed by the Mohawk, Oneida, Onondaga, Cayuga, and Seneca tribes between 1400 and 1500. The Tuscarora joined the confederacy in 1722.

longhouse—the traditional barn-shaped dwelling of the Iroquois. An average longhouse was 25 feet wide, 80 feet long, and housed about ten families.

Longhouse Religion—the Iroquois religion combining old and new beliefs that was established by the Seneca prophet Handsome Lake in 1799

missionary—a person who tries to persuade others to adopt his or her religion

Peacemaker—the legendary Iroquois figure who persuaded the Iroquois tribes to live together in peace

reservation—a piece of land set aside for the use of a particular group of American Indians in the United States

reserve—a tract of land set aside for the use of a particular group of Indians in Canada

Three Sisters—the three primary crops traditionally farmed by the Iroquois—corn, beans, and squash

wampum—white and purple shell beads that the Iroquois strung into belts to commemorate important events

To Find Out More

Books

Fradin, Dennis Brindell. *Hiawatha: Messenger of Peace*. New York: Margaret McElderry, 1992.

Gravelle, Karen. *Growing Up Where the Partridge Drums Its Wings: A Mohawk Childhood*. New York: Franklin Watts, 1997.

Graymont, Barbara. *The Iroquois*. New York: Chelsea House, 1988.

Hoyt-Goldsmith, Diane. *Lacrosse: The National Game of the Iroquois*. New York: Holiday House, 1998.

Levine, Ellen. *If You Lived with the Iroquois*. New York: Scholastic, 1999.

Shenandoah, Joanne. *Skywoman: Legends of the Iroquois.* Santa Fe: Clear Light Publishing, 1998.

Organizations and Online Sites

Ganondagan
P.O. Box 113
1488 State Route 444
Victor, NY 14564-0113
http://www.ganondagan.org
Visit the Ganondagan State Historic Site and see a replica of a seventeenth-century Seneca longhouse. The site also has three marked trails where you can learn about the Seneca Indians that once lived there.

Iroquois Indian Museum
http://www.iroquoismuseum.org
This tribal museum site features photographs of contemporary Iroquois life and art as well as historical information in its "electronic longhouse."

Oneida Indian Nation
http://www.oneida-nation.net
The New York Oneida's official site provides cultural information (including traditional recipes and audio files of the Oneida language) and news of its land-claim suit against New York State.

Seneca-Iroquois National Museum
794-814 Broad Street
P.O. Box 442
Salamanca, NY 14779
http://www.senecamuseum.org
Visitors to this museum can see traditional Iroquois crafts, artifacts, and modern artwork as well as special exhibits.

The Seneca Nation of Indians
http://www.sni.org
Read the Canandaigua Treaty of 1794 and learn more about Seneca Indians from this online site.

The Tuscarora School
http://www.tuscaroraschool.org
Discover from this site more about Tuscarora language, culture, and food.

A Note on Sources

There has been more written about the Iroquois than about any other American Indian group. I found a good starting point in the essays about the Iroquois Confederacy and individual Iroquois tribes in volume 15 of the Smithsonian's *Handbook of North American Indians*. Other brief general studies are two books simply titled *The Iroquois*—one by anthropologist Dean R. Snow, the other by historian Barbara Graymont.

Several excellent books deal with specific periods of Iroquois history. For the crucial Revolutionary War era, I relied on Barbara Graymont's *The Iroquois in the American Revolution*. For more recent history, I found particularly useful Laurence M. Hauptman's *Iroquois Struggle for Survival: World War II to Red Power*. An interesting take on contemporary times can be found in *Iroquois Culture and Commentary* (Clear Light Publishers, 2000), a collection of writings by the Mohawk journalist Doug George-Kanentiio.

—*Liz Sonneborn*

Index

Numbers in *italics* indicate illustrations.

61

About the Author

Liz Sonneborn is a writer and an editor, living in Brooklyn, New York. A graduate of Swarthmore College, she specializes in books about the history and culture of American Indians and the biographies of noteworthy people in American history. She has written more than twenty books for children and adults, including *A to Z of Native American Women* and *The New York Public Library's Amazing Native American History*.